December Journal Jumpstarts

A Month of Creative Writing Prompts

Written by
Cindy Barden

Editors: Barbara G. Hoffman and Michael Batty

Cover and Interior Design: Good Neighbor Press, Inc.

Illustrator: Chris Nye

FS112133 December Journal Jumpstarts

All rights reserved—Printed in the U.S.A.
23740 Hawthorne Boulevard
Torrance, CA 90505-5927

Notice! Pages may be reproduced for classroom or home use only, not for commercial resale. No part of this publication may be reproduced for storage in a retrieval system or transmitted in any form or by any means—electronic, mechanical, recording, etc.—without the prior permission of the publisher. Reproduction of these materials for an entire school or school system is strictly prohibited.

Copyright © 2000 Frank Schaffer Publications, Inc.

Table of Contents
December

Introduction 1
Hollow Moon 2
Blue 3
Progress 4
Pet Speak 5
Doing the Right Thing 6
Favorite Clothes 7
President Me 8
Three Important Qualities 9
Interests 10
Wheel Out the Welcome Wagon 11
Prize 12
Bonus 13
Windows of Wonder 14
Savor the Flavor 15
Double Animals 16
National Computer Day 17
Comic Strip 18
Super Saturdays 19
Special Person, Special Gift 20
Winter Wonderland 21
At the End of the Rainbow 22
Holiday Traditions 23
Winter Vacation 24
Daydreams 25
Winter Storm 26
Supersonic Travel 27
Underground City 28
Favorite Fiction 29
The End of Another Year 30

© Frank Schaffer Publications, Inc.   FS112133 December Journal Jumpstarts

Introduction

An empty journal is filled with infinite possibilities.

Writing regularly in a journal helps us to develop our imaginations, encourages us to express our thoughts, feelings, and dreams, and provides a way to communicate experiences in words and pictures. Many students feel frustrated when asked to keep a journal. They may not be sure of what to write, or they may be intimidated by a blank sheet of paper. Even professional writers occasionally face "writer's block." The Journal Jumpstarts series provides ideas and suggestions for daily journal entries. Each book contains 29 jumpstarts. You could give each student a photocopy of the same page or provide a variety of pages and allow students to choose their own topics. You may have students who will be able to sit and write without jumpstarts. At times students may prefer to express their thoughts through drawings or with a combination of drawings and writing. Be encouraging!

Through making regular entries in journals, students become more observant of themselves and the world around them. Journal writing on a regular basis strengthens students' attention spans and abilities to focus. Keeping journals promotes self-esteem because students are doing something for themselves—not for grades or in competition with others. A journal can become an essential friend, a confidante in times of personal crisis.

Encourage students to get into the journal habit by setting aside writing time every day at about the same time, such as first thing in the morning or shortly before lunch. Share their journal time by writing in your own journal. What better way to encourage a good habit than by example!

Note: Assure students that what they write is confidential. Provide a safe, secure place for students to store their journals. Respect their privacy, as you would expect your privacy to be respected—read their journals by invitation only.

Name _____ Date _____

Hollow Moon

Pretend that astronauts discover that the inside of the moon is hollow. Write about what they might find inside.

Name _____ Date _____

Blue

Write about your favorite blue thing and why you like it.

Name _____ Date _____

Progress

You may have set goals for yourself for the school year, such as reading 25 books, learning four new playground games, or keeping a daily journal. How much have you accomplished to meet your goals? Write about how you are going to accomplish them.

Name _____ Date _____

Pet Speak

What if you had a pet that could talk? What might it say to you? What would you ask it?

Name _____ Date _____

Doing the Right Thing

You probably know somebody who always tells the truth and who stands up for what he or she believes is right, even when it is hard to do the right thing. Write about that person and how you feel about his or her actions.

_____
_____
_____
_____
_____
_____
_____
_____
_____
_____
_____
_____
_____
_____
_____
_____
_____

Name _____ Date _____

Favorite Clothes

Write about your favorite piece of clothing or outfit. Describe why you like it.

Name _____ Date _____

President Me

Imagine being president for a day. As president, suggest a new law. Write your new law and describe why you are suggesting it.

_____
_____
_____
_____
_____
_____
_____
_____
_____
_____
_____
_____
_____

Name _____ Date _____

Three Important Qualities

Write the three most important qualities that you think a teacher should have and tell why you think those qualities are important.

_____
_____
_____
_____
_____
_____
_____
_____
_____
_____
_____
_____
_____
_____
_____
_____
_____
_____
_____

Name _____ Date _____

Interests

Think about things that you are good at or that interest you. Write about two or three of these things and describe what makes you good at them or why you like them.

Name _____   Date _____

Wheel Out the Welcome Wagon

Write about things that you can do to make someone new to your school or neighborhood feel welcome. If you've ever gone out of your way to welcome someone, write about it.

Name _____   Date _____

Prize

If you could win a prize for anything you wanted, what would you like to win a prize for? It could be for something you made or something you did.

Name _____ Date _____

Bonus

What would you do if you had $100 right now and could spend it in any way you wanted? Describe what you would do with the money and how much each item that you bought might cost.

_____

_____

_____

_____

_____

_____

_____

_____

_____

_____

_____

_____

_____

_____

_____

Name _____ Date _____

Windows of Wonder

Pretend that you have a window on your head that lets people see into your mind. Describe what people might see if they look through the window.

_____
_____
_____
_____
_____
_____
_____
_____
_____
_____
_____
_____
_____
_____
_____

Name _____   Date _____

Savor the Flavor

Write about your favorite flavor and why you like it. Try to describe how it tastes to you.

Name _____ Date _____

Double Animals

Many creatures from mythology and folklore combine the features of several animals. From Greek mythology, for example, the griffin was a combination of a lion and an eagle.

Pretend that you could combine two animals to make a new one. Which two animals would you choose? What would you call the new animal? What could it do?

_____
_____
_____
_____
_____
_____
_____
_____
_____
_____
_____
_____
_____
_____
_____
_____

Name _____ Date _____

National Computer Day

Computers have become very important to us. If we made up a holiday in honor of computers, how might we celebrate it? Describe activities, foods, or parties or make up a song.

Name _____ Date _____

Comic Strip

If you wrote a comic strip for the daily newspaper, what (or who) would it be about? What would you call it? Write a story for the main character(s).

Name _____ Date _____

Super Saturdays

Write about Saturdays at home. What do you like most about Saturdays? What do you like least?

Name _____ Date _____

Special Person, Special Gift

Think about someone special to you. What would be the best gift in the whole world for that person? Describe the person and the gift. Explain why that gift would be important to that person.

_____
_____
_____
_____
_____
_____
_____
_____
_____
_____
_____
_____
_____
_____
_____
_____
_____
_____

Name _____ Date _____

Winter Wonderland

Describe a wonderful winter scene. Include the sights, smells, tastes, sounds, and feel of your winter wonderland.

_____
_____
_____
_____
_____
_____
_____
_____
_____
_____
_____
_____
_____
_____
_____
_____
_____
_____

Name _____ Date _____

At the End of the Rainbow

You've been following a rainbow and are almost at the end. Describe what you find when you get there.

_____
_____
_____
_____
_____
_____
_____
_____
_____
_____
_____
_____
_____
_____
_____
_____

© Frank Schaffer Publications, Inc.

Name _____ Date _____

Holiday Traditions

Most families have holiday traditions. Write about holiday traditions that you and your family observe. Describe why they are important to you.

Name _____   Date _____

Winter Vacation

Write about some of the things you will do during winter vacation. Will you go somewhere? Will you see anyone special?

_____

_____

_____

_____

_____

_____

_____

_____

_____

_____

_____

_____

_____

_____

_____

_____

_____

Name _____ Date _____

Daydreams

When do you usually daydream? What kinds of things do you think about while you are daydreaming?

Name _____ Date _____

Winter Storm

Pretend that you are at home during a winter storm.
What do you see through the windows?
What do you hear?

Name _____   Date _____

Supersonic Travel

Pretend that you have built the fastest airplane in the world. Write about where you would go and what you would do.

_____
_____
_____
_____
_____
_____
_____
_____
_____
_____
_____
_____
_____
_____
_____
_____
_____
_____

Name _____   Date _____

Underground City

Pretend that you find the entrance to an underground city. Who lives there? What does it look like?

Name _____ Date _____

Favorite Fiction

Do you like mysteries? Science fiction and fantasy? Adventure stories? Write about your favorite type of fiction and tell why you like it.

Name _____ Date _____

The End of Another Year

Describe how this last year has been for you. Include the two best and two worst events of the year. What do you hope will happen next year?